Dear Family,

What's the best way to help your child love reading?

Find good books like this one to share—and read together!

Here are some tips.

● **Take a "picture walk."** Look at all the pictures before you read. Talk about what you see.

● **Take turns.** Read to your child. Ham it up! Use different voices for different characters, and read with feeling! Then listen as your child reads to you, or explains the story in his or her own words.

● **Point out words as you read.** Help your child notice how letters and sounds go together. Point out unusual or difficult words that your child might not know. Talk about those words and what they mean.

● **Ask questions.** Stop to ask questions as you read. For example: "What do you think will happen next?" "How would you feel if that happened to you?"

● **Read every day.** Good stories are worth reading more than once! Read signs, labels, and even cereal boxes with your child. Visit the library to take out more books. And look for other JUST FOR YOU! BOOKS you and your child can share!

The Editors

For my nephew, Evan Orlandi, and his amazing mom, Marcia.
Lights out, ya'll!
—ASM

For my little sister Sue, with love.
—NT

Text copyright © 2004 by Angela Shelf Medearis.
Illustrations copyright © 2004 by Nicole Tadgell.
Produced for Scholastic by COLOR-BRIDGE BOOKS, LLC, Brooklyn, NY
All rights reserved. Published by SCHOLASTIC INC.
JUST FOR YOU! is a trademark of Scholastic Inc.

Library of Congress Cataloging-in-Publication Data

Medearis, Angela Shelf, 1956-
    Lights out! / by Angela Shelf Medearis ; illustrated by Nicole Tadgell.
        p. cm.—(Just for you! Level 1)
    Summary: At bedtime, a young girl enjoys looking out her window and then creates a
puppet show with shadows on the wall.
    ISBN 0-439-56868-4
    [1. Bedtime—Fiction. 2. Shadows—Fiction. 3. Puppet theater—Fiction. 4. African
Americans—Fiction. 5. Stories in rhyme.] I. Tadgell, Nicole, 1969- ill. II. Title. III. Series.

PZ8.3.M551155Li 2004
[E]—dc22   2004004833
10 9 8 7 6 5   08
            Printed in the U.S.A. 23 • First Scholastic Printing, April 2004

Lights Out!

by Angela Shelf Medearis
Illustrated by Nicole Tadgell

▲▲▲▲ JUST FOR YOU!™ ▲▲▲▲
▲▲ Level 1 ▲▲

"Good night, sleep tight!"
Daddy tucks me in.

Out go the lights.
Now the fun begins!

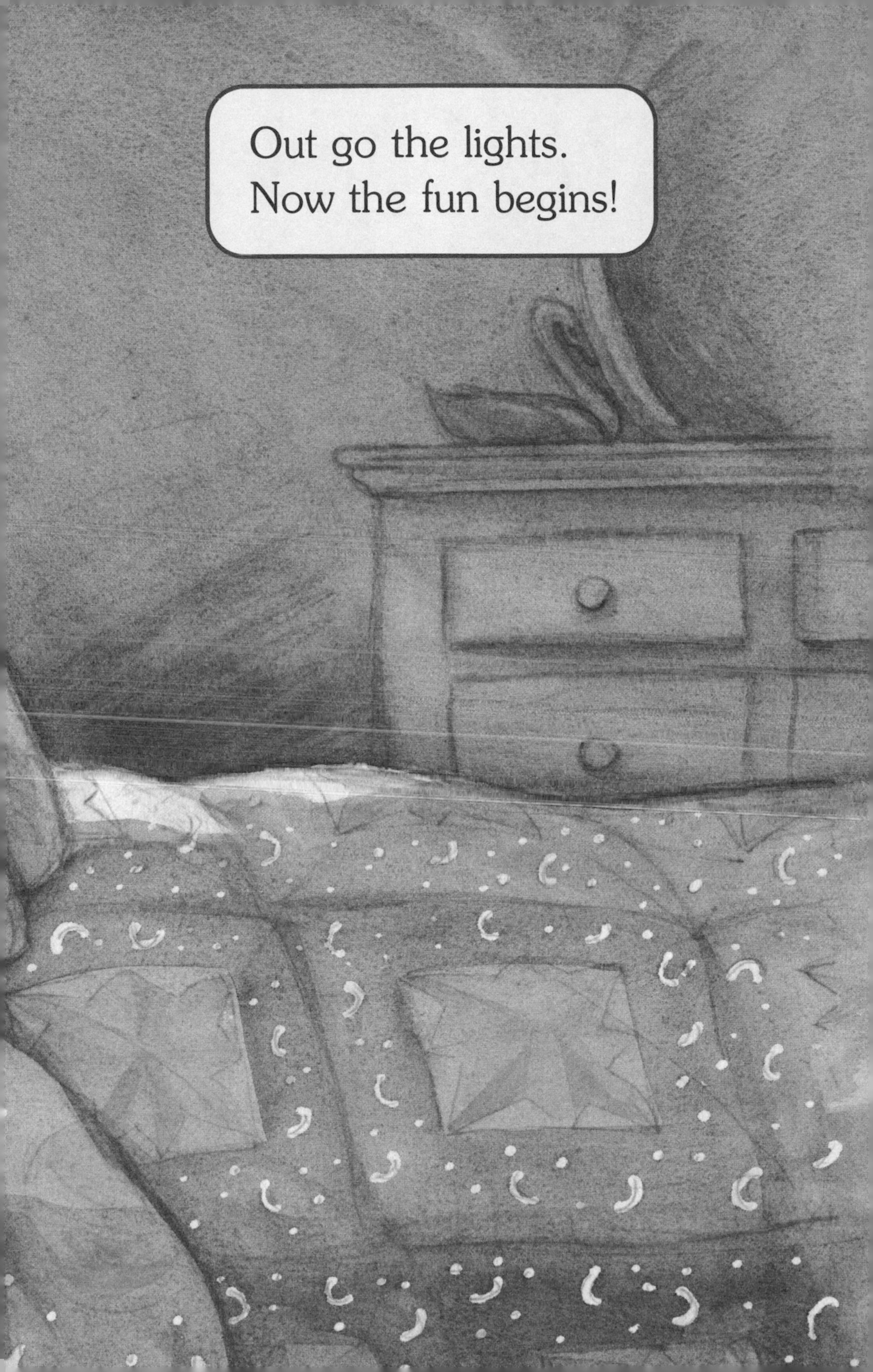

I know I should stay in bed at night, but I like to look at the city lights.

The dark clouds roll by.
The moon climbs in the sky.

A cool wind blows in.
On the street below,
trees sway and bend.

Stars shine brightly,
way up high,
twinkling like fireflies.

Cars and trucks
sing a rumbling song.

I snap my fingers
and hum along.

When city lights begin to glow,
I put on a puppet show.

Shadow rabbits, big and small,
hop, hop, hop across my wall.

A shadow duck swims slowly by.
I wave my hands to make it fly.

I dance and spin in the shadowy light.
Then playtime is over for the night.

I stretch and yawn.
My mouth opens wide.

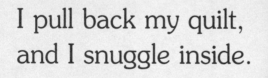

I pull back my quilt,
and I snuggle inside.

Slowly, slowly,
sleep creeps in.

Tomorrow I'll play
with the shadows again.

"Lights out!"

Here are some fun things for you to do.

YOUR Bedtime Rhyme

The girl's daddy says, "Good night, sleep tight."

Tight rhymes with **night**.

Do you know any more words that rhyme with night? ▲

Use some to make up your own bedtime rhyme!

Outside YOUR Window

The girl can see the city lights.

What can YOU see from your window?

She can hear cars and trucks.

What can YOU hear outside your window?

Draw a picture to show what YOU can see.

Write a sentence to tell what YOU can hear.

▲ Some rhyming words: bite, bright, fight, kite, light, might, quite, right, sight, tonight, white

A Puppet for YOU

You can make
a puppet, too.

Draw a little rabbit.
Cut it out.

Tape your rabbit
to a pencil
or your finger.

Make YOUR rabbit
hop, hop, hop!

▲▲▲▲TOGETHER TIME ▲▲▲▲

Make some time to share ideas about the story with your young reader! Here are some activities you can try. There are no right or wrong answers!

Talk About It: Ask your child, "Do you think the girl's father knows that she doesn't go right to sleep after he tucks her in? Do you think she puts on a puppet show every night?" What happens in your home at bedtime? Talk about what you and your child like to do when it's time to say good night.

Try This: Have your own shadow puppet show! First darken the room. Then use a small lamp or flashlight to shine a light on a wall. Have your child sit in between the light and the wall and use cut-out paper puppets (or his or her hands) to make a shadow duck or rabbit. Together, make up a story about where the shadow puppets are going as they hop, swim, or fly across your wall.

Act It Out: Reread the story aloud. This time, point out the action words (verbs) that tell how the girl moves: *snap, wave, dance, spin, stretch, yawn,* and *snuggle*. You and your child can act out these movements as you read!

Meet the Author

ANGELA SHELF MEDEARIS says, "When I was little, I shared a room with my sister. Every night, after our parents tucked us in, I got up to play. I would make up games, stories, and puppet shows as I watched the shadows move around the room. My nightly playtimes never bothered my sister. She could sleep through anything!"

Angela was born in Virginia. Her father was in the Air Force and the family moved often. In each place, Angela had to get used to a new home, a new school, and new friends. Angela remembers that visiting the library and finding favorite books to read made adjusting to a new place easier. Today she writes the kind of books she longed to find in the library when she was a child. She has written more than 70 books and won many awards for her work. Angela lives in Austin, Texas, with her husband Michael. Her other book in the JUST FOR YOU! series is *Singing for Dr. King*.

Meet the Artist

NICOLE TADGELL says, "Whenever I work on a new book, I find myself pretending to be the main character. I had fun being the little girl in this story. I guess I never really "grew up" inside. Even though I don't live in the city, I have visited cities—and I used many nighttime photographs for reference. While drawing and painting, I spent a lot of time in my studio at night, studying how the moonlight moved around the room, and playing with shadow puppets. I designed the quilt on the little girl's bed. I made her doll, too!"

Nicole grew up on Long Island, in New York, and graduated from Wheaton College. She now lives in Spencer, Massachusetts, with her husband Mark and their two border terriers. Nicole is also the illustrator of *A Day With Daddy* by Nikki Grimes, a JUST FOR YOU! Book; the "Joe Joe in the City" series by Jean Alicia Elster; and *Fatuma's New Cloth* by Leslie Bulion.